WRITE WAY

A believer's guide to effective communication

Contributing editors:
Hal Donaldson, Ken Horn, Randy Hurst, John W. Kennedy, Kirk Noonan, Scott Harrup

Pentecostal Evangel Books
Published by Gospel Publishing House

02-3034

Special recognition to the staff of *Today's Pentecostal Evangel*:
Connie Cross, Jodi Harmon, Keith Locke, Matt Key, Ron
Kopczick, Ashli O'Connell, Isaac Olivarez, Jena Schaumburg
and Marc McBride

Cover design by Keith Locke.

Library of Congress Control Number 2003108046
International Standard Book Number 0-88243-693-7
Printed in the United States of America

Contents

About the Authors

Hal Donaldson is editor in chief of *Today's Pentecostal Evangel*.

Ken Horn is managing editor of *Today's Pentecostal Evangel*.

Scott Harrup and Kirk Noonan are associate editors of *Today's Pentecostal Evangel*.

Randy Hurst is commissioner of evangelism for the Assemblies of God.

John W. Kennedy is news editor of *Today's Pentecostal Evangel*.

Foreword

I don't especially enjoy the task of writing. Most people don't. It can be an exhausting and stressful exercise: meeting deadlines, struggling to find the right word, and filling wastepaper baskets with failed attempts. So, if writing is such a hardship, why do we do it?

We write because we love to create. We enjoy communicating Truth and helping people discover Truth. The frustration that comes along with writing is a small price to pay to move the hearts and minds of people.

We do not have to love the mechanics of writing to be good writers. But every good writer must be willing to persevere and make sacrifices for the sake of communicating to readers. It requires willpower to sit down at a computer and begin the creative process. It takes more willpower to shape your work into a masterpiece. It takes even more willpower to take what you think is a masterpiece and turn it into something even better.

Most of the time I don't have enough willpower. As a result, I have to ask God to give me a desire and a willingness to pay the price necessary for excellent writing.

It's my prayer that this book will give you practical insights into the world of writing and let you know you are not alone in your struggles to write. But, most importantly, it will remind you that you're never writing alone. The Holy Spirit is with you and wants to be your partner in the creative process.

Hal Donaldson
Editor in Chief
Today's Pentecostal Evangel

1

Spirit-led Writing

By Hal Donaldson

Have you ever had an encounter with the Holy Spirit while sitting in front of your computer? Have you wept because you knew the Holy Spirit inspired something you had just written? Have you stopped to thank God for speaking to you as you were writing; and, before you knew it, you were speaking in tongues? If not, these are rewarding experiences God wants you to have as a writer.

I'm not suggesting that these experiences will guarantee that a person is an anointed, gifted writer. But I believe the Holy Spirit wants to play an active role in what we write—whether we're a beginner or a veteran.

Let's face it, each time you sit down to write is not going to be an "Upper Room" experience. Most of the time, writing is a rigorous exercise filled with frustration and the need for perseverance. For some it is a form of spiritual warfare. But I've found writing is much easier when I'm in communion with God and I'm leaning on the inspiration of the Holy Spirit.

Anointed writing is synonymous with hearing from God and being inspired by the Holy Spirit. So, what can we do to ensure that we hear from God? How do we invite the Holy Spirit to influence our writing?

Examine your motive. Writing Christians are believers at worship. It's easy to think of ourselves as ministers/influencers with a pen in our hand or a computer on our lap. But, in reality, first and foremost, we are worshipers. Our writing is an act of worship. So, why do we write? We write for God's pleasure; then, second, we write to bless others and ourselves. There are two types of writers: those who write for God and those who write for themselves.

As a young journalist I traveled to El Salvador to write a magazine article. I rubbed shoulders with several self-serving writers/reporters from major networks and newspapers. They were disregarding the truth in order to propel their careers. Their reporting techniques and dog-eat-dog philosophy reminded me that, as Christians, our primary purpose in writing is to glorify and serve God. When it comes to art forms and creative endeavors, it's easy to begin assuming some of the credit for what God is accomplishing through us.

Many Christian writers struggle in this area. Subconsciously they become more concerned with seeing their name in print than seeing God's name proclaimed. They're more focused on their careers than on winning the lost.

I challenge you to ask God to give you a passion for

lost people. When you have that passion, you won't need to worry about your motive; you will write out of that passion. The question you should ask is not how you can get published, but how God can use your writing skills to reach the lost and inspire believers.

The church is experiencing a dearth of writing prophets who use their writing to arrest the attention of readers who are continually being secularized. Perhaps God is calling you to be a prophetic voice through the written page — a medium that can reach the masses. Today people like Charles Finney, John and Charles Wesley and Charles Price are still reaching the world through their writing. Will the evangelists of today still be heard 30 years from now, if the Lord tarries?

Prepare. My college professor said, "Good writing is never accidental. It is a deliberate attempt to communicate ideas, facts or impressions." The same can be said with one's quest to become a writer who is inspired by the Holy Spirit. Yes, it helps to have an education and to study the craft, but anointed writing requires daily preparation.

Consider following these three steps daily:

1. *Pray.* Perhaps you have a quiet room where you go to write. Your effectiveness in your writing room will depend on what happens in your prayer closet. In that prayer closet you should pray about your writing. Pray (1) that God would give you a good idea for your book or article; (2) that He would grant you the creative clarity to communicate that idea; (3) that He would open the doors to have the work published. Often, we pray for step three before we pray for the idea or the Lord's

help in creative communication.

2. *Read the Bible and the newspaper.* Columnist Cal Thomas wrote: "There are two things I read every morning—my Bible and the *New York Times*—so I know what each side is doing."

God wants us to be informed about our world. To be an effective, relevant writer you must be Christ-conscious and world-informed.

3. *Look for opportunities to serve others.* Some of the greatest writers—Ernest Hemingway, C.S. Lewis, Max Lucado—often write out of personal experience. Being a writer is not a license to become a "computer hermit." Without ongoing ministry experiences a writer eventually loses his/her well of ideas. How can we write about lost souls and evangelism if we isolate ourselves from the lost? How can we write about servanthood if we never serve a brother or sister? A writer is on a life-long journey looking for deeper truths, new stories to tell. If your journey has stalled, look for a place to serve.

Author Ethel Herr encourages writers to "open their senses" and their hearts to God's prodding, to people, to human need, to their own emotions and needs. She challenges us to be aware of our dreams, fears and frustrations; because, if we're feeling or facing something, others are too. In these personal experiences we find topics.

An important element in this is obedience. We can't expect to have an anointing if we're not tithing, if we're mistreating a spouse, or if we're gossiping about our pastor. I like to paraphrase Matthew 15:18: "What is in my heart comes out of my printer."

As you give the Holy Spirit freedom to influence every area of your life, you will experience benefits that will breathe life into your writing.

The Holy Spirit will give you courage and boldness. As a young reporter, I was sent to New York City to interview Dan Rather and John Chancellor. Beforehand, I prayed in my hotel room: "Dear Lord, You made this possible. You're going in there with me. Take away my fear. Give me courage and boldness." And He did. The interviews were outstanding.

We have access to that power whether conducting interviews, researching, talking to an editor, writing or submitting an article for consideration.

The Holy Spirit will give you determination. When you write something you believe in, you won't accept no for an answer. You won't be discouraged by rejection slips. You'll try again ... and again ... and again.

Some would-be writers are like the rich young ruler in Matthew 19 who asked Jesus, "What must I do to have eternal life?" Jesus said, "Go sell what you have and come and follow Me." When the man was asked to pay a price to follow Jesus, he decided the price was too great and he walked away. Some would-be writers are not willing to pay the price spiritually. They don't understand that writing is a form of service; it is ministry.

Some ask, "What must I do to become an anointed writer?" Anointed writing requires denying self. It requires a decision to put God first in everything. And that determination, like any other spiritual discipline, is ultimately a gift from God.

The Holy Spirit will give you opportunities to influence lives. Look for opportunities to be published. Send out résumés. Contact an agent. But, ultimately, God is the publicist you need. He is looking for writers who will make themselves available to influence the church and society.

In 1776 half of the literature published was religious in nature or published by religious groups. But, many of the publications and publishers began to wane in significance because they began dealing with issues that weren't pertinent to readers. Anointed writers will be relevant and effective.

The Holy Spirit will expose hindrances to good writing. In Genesis 26 Isaac is in the desert and he's thirsty. He decides to travel to the wells his father Abraham had dug earlier. He journeys to the wells only to discover they have been filled with debris. He knows the water is there. So he digs out the debris, and life-giving water begins to flow and his thirst is quenched.

Debris in our lives may be obstructing the flow of the Holy Spirit, hindering His inspiration in our writing. It may be sin, misplaced priorities, impure motives. These obstructions must be removed so we can be the writers God wants us to be.

As writers, we must reclaim our position of influence, and that will only happen when we are anointed to write. Anointed writers will be relevant and effective. There is power in Pentecostal pens.

2

Nuts and Bolts

By Hal Donaldson

Most editors of Christian publications can tell this story. A freelance submission is received with a cover letter from the writer outlining the subject and the circumstances that brought about its creation.
Somewhere in the letter the writer explains, "God gave me this idea. I pray it will be a blessing to your readers." Unspoken, but equally apparent, is the writer's belief that his or her article, testimony, short story or poem will automatically be published now that its divine inspiration has been revealed.

God does inspire believers with ideas for writing projects. But that inspiration does not negate the writer's need to apply the disciplines of the writing craft in order to flesh out an idea.

Following are some reasons that editors and publishers reject manuscripts.

The content is flawed. Every writer should ask:

"Would people be willing to pay $1 to read my article if it were the only article in the magazine I'm sending it to?" That's the writer's "$1 rule," and it can easily be extrapolated to a "$15 rule" for a book. Your evaluation of how well your article would stand on its own is a good indicator of whether or not you have a good subject and adequate content.

The manuscript isn't focused. It tries to say too much on too many subjects. For example, it's impossible within one article to deal with everything concerning parenting. Choose a slant—family devotions—and stick with it. Don't wander off into other subjects, such as discipline or peer pressure.

The content is not interesting, even though the subject itself is. Perhaps you decide to write on prayer. You can't simply tell the reader to pray. If you don't write in an interesting and creative way, even an important subject like prayer will be rejected. Look for fresh ways—anecdotes, illustrations, etc.—to communicate a popular theme.

The lead paragraph is stale. The opening paragraph may be all the time an editor can give your manuscript. Grab the editor. Grab the reader with a sentence or two that come alive.

The application to the reader's life is missing. Generally, articles should provoke emotion or a response from readers to pray or to witness to their neighbor, for example.

The content has a negative slant or bitter tone. Typically editors do not want their pages used to attack or condemn. If a writer is going to deal with a problem, he or she should offer some reasonable solution and couch the article's language in redemptive, as opposed to judgmental, terms.

The writer spends too much time justifying the piece. This is called "throat clearing." If you find the real lead paragraph four paragraphs into your piece, cut out the first three to get right to the subject.

The audience is misunderstood, so the article does not meet the readers' needs. A world-renowned cardiologist may write a well-crafted article on the symptoms of heart disease. But if she submits that article to the editor of a lawn and garden magazine, it isn't going to be published. Writers must accurately assess a publication's audience before they submit their material.

Magazines don't just entertain; they meet a critical need in their audience. Beyond evaluating the subjects covered in your target publication, ask yourself what that magazine is trying to accomplish in people's lives.

Today's Pentecostal Evangel, for example, is not just looking for 10-minute sermonettes, although you may see such items included on occasion. The *Evangel* is looking for articles that touch on the everyday experiences of believers and help them cope with life's challenges through the power of Jesus Christ. Think of the readers, because the subscribers own the magazine.

The article is more of a weapon than a blessing. These are cases when an article will speak to the magazine's audience, but will be so offensive that editors don't want to deal with the mail and phone calls they'll get if they print it. Choose your words carefully. Remember, "A word aptly spoken is like apples of gold in settings of silver" (Proverbs 25:11). Encourage rather than berate.

The style undercuts the message. Style is difficult to quantify or describe. It is very subjective. An anecdote that seems warmhearted to one editor may strike another as maudlin. Understand that every editor is going to use his or her subjective sense of style when evaluating your work.

The article is too preachy. You don't want your article to read like a sermon, even when you are presenting biblical truths. Someone said, "Preaching shouts a message, while writing shares insights into truth."

The article is riddled with clichés. "Fast as a rabbit," "sings like an angel," "cute as a button" … the list of worn-out expressions is too long to consider here. When writing for the Christian market, also be wary of religious jargon that will be meaningless or misinterpreted by an unsaved reader.

The manuscript is 1,000 words and is worthy of 250. Keep an eye out for components in your writing that are too long. Do your sentences drag? Do your paragraphs look like intimidating blocks of copy?

Good sermons move. They have action, illustrations and well-paced timing. Likewise, writing must not get bogged down. Maintain a momentum that will draw the reader to your conclusion. The difference between a good sermon and good writing, however, is that the tools you use while speaking are not available to you as a writer. You're not there when people read your article. You can't make eye contact or interject meaningful pauses or facial expressions. The emphasis you may hear in your head when writing out certain words in your article will not be automatically apparent to that distant reader. But the equivalent of all of those helpful points can come across through organization and proper transitions.

The only way you are going to create a polished finished product is through the hard work of outlines and rewriting. Three drafts are a minimum. You will need a skeleton to get your ideas onto paper. A first draft can create the smooth wording and transitions you need. A technical edit and final draft can catch the mistakes you would never want to slip onto an editor's desk.

The misuse of grammar weakens the message. Editors don't want to devote their time and energy to an extensive rewrite of your work. They expect your professionalism to carry the article and make their job one of fine-tuning. Have a friend read and edit your work before you submit it. Following the three-draft process will help you get over this hurdle.

The manuscript is filled with "telling" writing. Ask yourself: "Which is more effective—if I tell the reader, 'The dog was ugly,' or if I show it by describing the dog's fangs, scars, deformed ear and matted hair?" Allow your reader to come to his or her own conclusion. That's complimenting the reader, and it will strengthen your writing. Because of the brevity of most magazine articles, writers aren't able to be as descriptive, but the discipline is still a valuable principle. Show; don't tell.

The format screams "beginner writer." If your manuscript comes into an editorial office handwritten on a grocery bag, it won't see the light of day. That is an exaggeration, but a manuscript can turn an editor off in a variety of ways. If it is single spaced, if corrections are in the margins rather than retyped in the body of the text, if a near-empty ink cartridge results in faded print—these are red flags that will increase the chances of an editor only giving your piece a cursory look before stuffing it into your SASE. Your work needs to be neat and follow a standard manuscript article format.

Here is a grab bag of miscellaneous setbacks to successful publication.

1. Sometimes you'll submit an article on a subject that a magazine has already given adequate coverage. Be sure you have read several recent issues of any publication you are trying to work with. A query letter regarding the subject you have in mind can often save you unnecessary work.

2. Your topic may be dated. For example, unless you have found a little-known angle, you probably don't want to write another piece on 9/11.

3. Maybe an editor doesn't feel the author has the credentials to write on a specific subject. If, for example, you have chosen a complex issue concerning the law and you're not an attorney, your article will raise editorial doubts. Under such circumstances, be sure to include source documentation and justify your connection to the subject.

4. Some magazines are less likely to accept manuscripts that have already appeared in other publications. Be sure to read their writers guidelines and look for second-rights policies.

5. The article does not have a strong spiritual message or lacks scriptural basis. In the Christian market, this often becomes No. 1 on the list.

Roger Palms of the Billy Graham Evangelistic Association gives the following tips for including Scripture in your evangelistic writing:

1. Tell a Bible story and relate it to a modern-day situation.

2. Quote from the Bible.

3. Don't lead your article or book with a Scripture (preachy).

4. Identify Bible characters with people today.

5. Trace a word through the Bible.

6. Look for fresh approaches, such as anecdotes, to convey biblical topics.

7. Use Scripture to tell your testimony.

If you are a committed believer and you have dedicated your writing skills to the Lord, God will certainly give you ideas. The key is to be a good steward of those ideas and shape them with every creative tool at your disposal. Your discipline as a writer can make all the difference in whether or not the ideas the Lord gives you are published.

But remember that being published means dealing with human beings. Even if your article is well crafted and faithful to the inspiration you sense from the Holy Spirit, you may encounter an editor who has not caught that vision. Relating to editors is another critical component of the writer's life. The next chapter offers some insights on that subject.

3

Writers Are From Mars, Editors Are From Venus

By Hal Donaldson

A recent best-selling book discussed the differences between men and women and offered insights into overcoming those differences and developing relationships. Writers and editors certainly have their differences; but, if any publication is to succeed, they need to overcome differences and develop a relationship. Writers and editors can become a highly effective publishing team if they learn to communicate.

On the front end of a writer/editor relationship, it will be primarily up to the writer to establish lines of contact. An editor, most likely, will not know who you are or anything about your writing as you are starting out in the craft. But you can take steps to see your work receive the editorial attention you believe it deserves.

Communicating from Mars: What you can do for your editor

1. Submit a relevant, good topic. An editor will

21

overlook poor format and style and will invest time in your manuscript if the idea is striking.

2. Feature prominent, recognizable people. Or, tell someone's remarkable salvation testimony, or a gripping story of one's ministry activities. People are interested in reading about other people.

3. Have good photographs available to accompany the article. I remember receiving an article some years ago about an NBA player. The article was poorly written, but the photos were fabulous. So we bought both and did an extensive edit.

4. Communicate in your cover letter or query if you have extensive writing experience. But be honest and back up your claims. Cite the publication dates of the published articles you reference. Most editors look with a skeptical eye at a generic claim to have been published in "hundreds of magazines and journals."

5. Know the magazine. Have a general knowledge of what the magazine has and has not published over the last year. Study the writers guidelines. This is one of the ways you can compliment the editor, by showing that you have been involved as a reader.

6. Look for ways to personally touch base. Consider this point carefully. Periodic phone calls, e-mails or quick notes about your latest writing project (even if it is for another publication) can help keep your name in front of an editor. But overkill can backfire. If a magazine that interests you has rejected your material, don't give up, but keep your contact low-key. It never helps you to come across as desperate.

**7. Include subheads, a great title, and photo cut-

lines if you have them. In other words, make the editor's job as easy as you can. Know enough about the publication to have a general idea of the components of a typical layout. If you can supply some of those components from the front end, do so.

8. Relate to editors as business people. Their careers depend on their ability to sell magazines. If you have suggestions on how you can sell or distribute large quantities, let the editor know. For example, if you approached a Christian publication with an exclusive interview with Billy Graham and knew that the Billy Graham Evangelistic Association would purchase 5,000 copies, let the editor know.

9. Meet deadlines for assigned material. Turning in an assignment late could be the death knell of your relationship with an editor. Editors work on very rigid schedules and cannot afford to give you the luxury of procrastinating. Most will be understanding of a legitimate emergency, but few will give you a second chance to be lazy.

10. Volunteer for assignments. As your relationship with a publication grows, feel free to share article ideas with an editor and suggest ways in which you could create the finished product.

11. Consider submitting to nonreligious publications. In developing the writing talent God has given you, don't make the mistake of believing that all nonreligious publications are off limits. On the contrary, a Christian viewpoint can be the foundation for an article suitable for just about any publication. Use your biblical worldview to inform your piece on conservation or dating relationships or the repercussions of a recent world event. You don't need to include a single Scripture reference or give an altar call. Just present a Christian ethic in your analysis and creativity.

Communicating with the editor of a non-Christian publication calls for tact. If he or she believes you might use the publication as a pulpit, you won't see your material in print. Don't feel like you have to trumpet your religious convictions in your cover letter. Just offer a straightforward explanation of why you wrote, or propose to write, your article and the benefit you believe your piece would have for the magazine's readers.

Life on Venus: Your editor's view of the writing world

As a writer, you have responsibilities and goals. Editors do too. The more closely you can identify with an editor, the better your chances of eventually being published. For the purposes of this book, the focus here is on the editor of a denominational publication.

1. The editor must juggle the various roles of his or her magazine. The magazine establishes an image for the denomination, since it is the only contact, for most readers, with the larger church organization. It reports the denomination's direction and sets forth the priorities of church leadership. It also may call on a course of action from the readers and seek to rally them to a cause. These are all vital roles, and the magazine's effectiveness for the denomination and the kingdom of God hinges on how successfully editors can work with church leaders to create a common understanding of a magazine's mission and purpose.

Writers need to be aware of this larger mission and purpose and ask themselves if their proposal or article will contribute to those goals. This requires the writer to get outside of his or her small circle of church friends and gain a perspective of the larger church fellowship.

2. The editor must work cooperatively with church leadership while charting a course for the magazine. Editors have to answer for everything appearing in a magazine, including your article. They must justify the inclusion of each item before other levels of administration. Again, this means you need to be aware of the broader policies and positions of the sponsoring church behind a religious magazine.

3. Editors have a heart for the spiritual needs of readers. Editors, like writers, share in the mission of literary evangelism. If you are going to contribute to a church magazine, make sure you do so with a heart for souls. An editor who senses that you want to use a publication as just another citation on your résumé will be less than enthusiastic about seeing your name in the table of contents.

4. Editors want to give their readers excellence. Many editors are writers themselves, and feel good when they can give a fellow writer an opportunity to grow in their publication. But a good editor never lets that desire outweigh the responsibility to give the readers a good product. Ask yourself if your piece really merits the combined time invested by thousands of readers of a publication. Are you offering your best product for the greatest benefit to the most readers?

5. Editors want to communicate clearly with a diverse audience. People from all walks of life and all levels of spiritual maturity pick up a Christian magazine. When you write, don't make assumptions about your reader's biblical knowledge or spiritual frame of reference. This doesn't mean you insult your reader's intelligence. It means you write clearly and convincingly using the writing tools discussed earlier. Editors are looking for writers who are communicators. When they find them, they keep them in focus for additional assignments.

6. Editors strive to remain on the cutting edge. Christian publications cannot afford to be out of touch with current events and current publishing trends. If your target publication has a news section, keep an eye out for local or national news stories affecting the church or needing a Christian point of view. Contact the news editor of the magazine with your idea. Keep up-to-date on a magazine's design. Look for ways to connect your story ideas with new columns or features. If you have been a long-time reader of a publication, make sure your ideas are tied to the newest look in the magazine.

7. Editors want to trust their writers. As you build a relationship with an editor, you will find that you are given more liberties in the writing assignments that come your way. A first-time assignment to an untested writer often carries a list of requirements, and the creative possibilities are consequently held in check. As you keep the above points in focus and create material accordingly, your editor will trust your creative instincts. The day you receive a writing assignment that lists a deadline, a word count, and only a sentence or two on subject matter, consider yourself highly complimented. You've earned your editor's confidence. You've become part of a magazine's valued writing team. Now it's time to keep growing and look for another editor to begin the process with again.

4

Defeating Writer's Block

By Hal Donaldson

Few things are more intimidating to a writer than a blank sheet of paper or a blank computer screen. The hardest sentence in an article is often the first one; and, if a deadline is looming, the pressure to be creative can be at odds with the creative process. Books on writing offer practical tips to jumpstart ideas, but, as a Pentecostal writer, you have an option no secular book on writing will mention—the Holy Spirit. He is waiting for you to trust Him with your most cherished ideas.

Think who the Holy Spirit is. He is the Person in the Trinity who brought about the Bible, the greatest collection of writings in human history. Biography, history, poetry, theology—they are all there. Imagine partnering with the One who whispered to David the words of Psalm 23 or inspired John to pen the phrase, "For God so loved the world ... " (John 3:16).

Does this mean the Holy Spirit will lead you to write something of equal authority with Scripture? No, and that's the answer you expect if you're going to give credence to this chapter. But God's Spirit can inspire you to feats of creativity that will make scriptural truths come alive for your readers. Whether you write poems, devotionals, short stories or even novels, your creative energies, dedicated to the Spirit's service, can bring incredible results.

Start from a position of humility. Romans 8:26 says, "The Spirit helps us in our weakness." Self-help books often call for self-confidence, but never forget that your confidence is grounded in the Spirit's gifts invested in you.

In journalism school, my professors said often: "Ask the right questions." Staring at an empty page that must be filled with copy, most writers ask this question first: "What do I want to write?" The Spirit-led writer asks: "What does the Holy Spirit want me to write?"

So, how can the Holy Spirit influence your writing?

First, acknowledge that the Holy Spirit speaks. Sometimes we hear His voice; sometimes we don't. But be assured He is speaking … and listening. He is interested in what you write and how you write it. He wants to use your pen to communicate His message.

The question of what the Holy Spirit wants you to write is connected to three other questions.

Have I positioned my heart to hear the Spirit's voice?

Some people think it's enough that they spoke in tongues when they received the baptism in the Holy Spirit. From then on, they believe, they are anointed for whatever task God has for them. Once is not enough. Praying in the Spirit regularly helps position our hearts to receive from God. Praying in the Spirit is vital to anointed writing.

Spirit-led writers guard their hearts against sin. They can't harbor secret sins and expect to hear God's voice clearly. What's occurring in their private lives—good or bad—will ultimately influence their writing.

Keep your motives pure. Why are you writing? Do you have visions of autograph sessions, seeing your name on the *New York Times* best-seller list and making millions? Or, are you writing as unto the Lord?

You have three audiences: Sometimes you write to touch others; sometimes you write what become, in essence, love letters to God; sometimes you write to minister to yourself. Not everything you write is destined to be published. Why allow publishers alone to validate your writing? Write as unto the Lord.

Correctly positioning your heart requires that you have regular devotions, pray in the Spirit, overcome temptation and keep your motives pure.

What does God want me to write?

I used to think finding God's will was wearing a funnel on my head and allowing the Holy Spirit to pour in instructions. I've discovered that finding God's will is more conversational and interactive. It's asking God questions and then waiting for answers. For example, "Lord, I'd really like to write on the subject of marriage. Is that a topic I should consider?"

As you seek God, He will answer through circumstances or strong impressions. He will speak to you through experiences, impulses and ideas. God often uses my conversations on airplanes or exchanges with

my children to birth writing ideas in my mind.
Sometimes I'll be praying or reading the Bible or the
newspaper, and I'll get a strong impression that begins
to expand in my mind over the following days. A writing outline will develop. That's God speaking.

Be honest. How many times have you had something
you've wanted to write, but you never wrote it? If
someone asked you why you hadn't started the project,
you'd say, "I just haven't gotten around to it."

Possibly it's not God's timing for that subject to come
to fruition. He may have some additional principles or
truths He wants to teach you before you write it. But
it's also possible He wants you to write about that subject, but you're afraid of rejection or you're simply too
busy.

The biggest obstacle in my ability to hear God's
voice—to know what to write and how to write it—is
my busy lifestyle. I have to schedule solitude into my
schedule. If your schedule has taken control of your
life, slow down. Listen and observe the world around
you. That's how you discern what God wants you to
write.

Obedience is another factor. The Holy Spirit guides
those who have resolved to respond. He's not going to
give instructions that He knows you have resolved to
ignore.

How does God want me to write it?

Just because the Spirit is guiding your writing doesn't
mean the writing will come easily. Some of the most
important things you'll write will also be the most difficult. The enemy will fight against you.

When I'm having a difficult time writing, I use a

technique known as "stream of consciousness." I simply write the article straight through without getting hung up on exact wording or sentence structure. Then I go back and chisel away and buff the piece, so to speak. I'm not ignoring the Holy Spirit when I push through with that kind of determination. I'm just getting some ideas on to paper that He can help me evaluate. No one can edit an empty sheet of paper.

So, how does God want you to express yourself in your writing? Receiving the guidance of the Holy Spirit is not a passive exercise. You have to do your part to prepare. You have to read the works of good writers; you have to study techniques; you have to nurture your talents. Then you begin to create a catalog of writing styles and techniques that become a mental toolbox for the Spirit to employ. With these tools in place, when you ask the Holy Spirit for guidance, He can bring to your mind an expression, a technique, a writing style that will communicate.

Writers constantly try to build their readership and gain some momentum. The Holy Spirit knows exactly what you need to do to increase the visibility and effectiveness of your writing. Ask Him for a vision. Ask Him for the plan to achieve that vision.

Writers value communication. How you say something is as important as what you say. For Christian writers, the "what" is the gospel. You have the message of hope in Jesus Christ. But if you're not communicating and touching people where they are—in a way they can understand—you're not fulfilling the Great Commission.

Spirit-led writing is born out of a passion for God

and a burden for people. My prayer is that the Lord would stir in every writer reading these pages a desire for more of Him ... and a desire to see lives transformed.

5

Writing With Passion

By Ken Horn

Writers must be enthusiastic about the things they write about and transfer that passion to paper. That makes their writing convincing.

From an editor's view, a passionately written article that says something but is not top-notch writing is better than a well-written article that doesn't say much. If you have something to say, all that remains is getting into your subject and bringing life to it.

Everybody, including writers, should do two things: Do what you're good at and do what you enjoy. Don't force yourself into others' molds. Harder work is not necessarily better work. The most effective use of your time is using the gifts God has given you.

I like writing, but I don't like the discipline of writing. I've found that most of my best ideas flow from relaxed thinking. Always write ideas down when they come to you. Don't lose them. Read a lot in your areas of interest, respond to what you read, then create.

Writing and passion go together in two ways: Be passionate about writing itself, and be passionate about your subject material.

1. Passionate about writing. How do you get passion for writing? Read a lot … in areas you like, in areas you might like. Read writers you like. Ask yourself why you like them. Reading good writing helps to develop a passion to emulate it. Be careful though that writing does not become an end in itself. Good writing will always grab my attention; but if it goes nowhere I eventually get bored.

2. Passionate about your subject. You must have passion for what you write about. If you're not convinced, your readers probably won't be either.

Write out of your interest or expertise—if you're still passionate about it. Passion parallels emotion. God made people emotional beings. If they laugh or cry, they'll remember. Be sure to give them something to keep. A good story with a clear moral is more effective than a sermon.

There are two main components to writing: information and inspiration.

1. Sources of information

• *Documentaries:* Analogies or similes can be drawn from any interest you have, even though they don't directly apply to your topic. I've used everything from buffalo herds to a botched baseball play to make spiritual points.

• *Print media:* I'm always clipping something. If I have the impulse, I clip it. I've regretted not clipping something. A while back I found myself rummaging through the garbage for something I should have clipped earlier. Local stories are valuable because you may be the only one writing about them.

• *Internet:* You can clip good info from a Web page just as easily as from a periodical. (But be sure to note the source.)

• *Books:* Glean illustrations as you read.

• *Family, friends:* Try to benefit from their reading and experiences by making them aware of things you could use. My wife, Peggy, reads different books than I do. Occasionally she reads me a passage about something I'm interested in. I'll sometimes make a note and later incorporate it into an article.

• *Life:* Always be aware. Some of the little observations can provide the best illustrations. If it really interests you, the chances are it will interest readers.

• *Church:* This is an information hub with a wealth of material. Keep your eyes and ears open.

2. Sources of inspiration

• *Testimonies:* Traveling to report for the *Evangel*, we often get some of our best stories incidentally, after the reporting is over. There are people in your church with great testimonies. They may not get into print unless you write them.

• *People's stories:* Don't overlook the stories your friends and family tell. My Grandmother Corey went through the 1906 great San Francisco earthquake and fire. She told that story over and over, but I never wrote it down or recorded it. Now she's gone, and I'm a writer wishing I had notes about all the things she experienced. Instead I have just a vague memory.

• *God's creation:* Nature can be a terrific source of

inspiration. God's universe, though fallen, is still incredible.

• *Your own walk with the Lord:* Hopefully this will supply you with good devotional material. If it doesn't, then put aside your writing and work on your walk.

• *Feelings:* How you felt going through a trial, an illness, etc. The sense of wonder you experience gazing upon something of natural beauty. Record descriptive phrases, descriptive paragraphs, experiences. Describe how you feel, or how others said they felt.

Types of passionate writing are:

• Stories you were a part of

• Human-interest stories. If they gripped you, they'll grip others.

• Great news

Decide if you want to be controversial or provocative. If you have a negative message, be sure to leave the reader with hope, not just a challenge.

Some practices for putting passion on paper. Be sure you care about what you're writing. Then, do your best to show the readers you care. Be honest … with yourself and others. If you're not into it, success is a long shot. Be aware of the difference between passion and prejudice (a bias that makes you think a story is better than it is because the subject is close to you).

1. Record ideas immediately. I've gotten sermons and editorials in the shower—better than ones I labored over. Keep a pad by your bed; have one everywhere you go. Don't lose an idea. Keep files of descriptive phrases, anything that impresses you.

2. Develop thoughts instead of wasting time. I use flight time to write.

3. Think (meditate). When I pastored, I tried to write next Sunday's sermon on Monday morning. That way I could think about it all week. I got lots of fresh illustrations that way.

4. Be willing to have less-than-perfect first drafts. Write when inspired. Leave blanks, write words you know you'll never use—to expedite the thought process. Holding a high writing standard in early drafts can short circuit passion and cause you to lose content. Writing passionately usually means filling in the blanks later.

5. Write it your way (within reason). Don't try to be someone you're not. It can be a straightjacket if you don't let your own personality seep onto your pages.

6. Capture images that evoke passion. You can't be so passionate about your subject that you are unwilling to give up words to the editor's red line. My columns always start too long. Writers who don't want us to change anything are too difficult to work with. Do not be defensive about cuts—unless you don't want to keep writing for that publication.

Christian writers must have passion for God and the Word. It also helps to be passionate and knowledgeable about the publications you're submitting to. A clear understanding is better than flattery.

Ask yourself some questions. When I have time to day-dream, what do I think about? What do I look forward to on the weekend ... or vacation? Why do I like it? Will others care?

Your passion is transferable if you can relate it to others and you can make it breathe.

6

Writing to Change Lives

By Ken Horn

An inmate in an Oregon prison tossed some trash into a garbage can when he saw a crumpled magazine on top and his eye was drawn to the word "Oregon." I had written an editorial in the *Pentecostal Evangel* about some floods that occurred in Oregon, where I pastored before coming to Springfield, Mo. The inmate read that article, then continued to read the entire magazine. It culminated in his prayer to receive Jesus Christ as Lord and Savior.

Every day in our offices we receive salvation coupons from those who have accepted the Lord after reading a *Pentecostal Evangel*. Being a former pastor and missionary evangelist, I consider this the most important result of producing the magazine. In response to those coupons, each year nearly 1,800 individuals receive follow-up materials on the new Christian life, and churches in their communities are contacted. The *Evangel* also receives countless letters from people whose lives have been touched in some way by something written in our pages.

Christian writing is more than entertainment; it can make a difference in people's lives. It is not a desk job; it's ministry. It is the Christian writer's ministry to grip the reader in order to make a positive change in his or her life.

I don't write to impress or to make a living. I write to touch lives. That motivation influences everything that I write.

You need to know why you want to write. Ask yourself that question now. Identifying your motivation for writing is foundational to shaping how you write. Besides knowing why you write, you need to know what kind of writing best fulfills your reasons for writing. Ask yourself that as well.

I'm kidded by our staff about always having a "sermon" at the end of my editorials. I'm a preacher at heart. When I taught systematic theology in college, I still considered myself a minister and attempted to minister to the students. Writing is the same. Everything you do as a Christian bears some kind of fruit.

You may be a storyteller or a teacher or a poet. Writing styles are as individual as writers. Great Christian writing is effective ministry—even if it is fiction or light reading. The many kinds of Christian writing all contribute to the spread of the gospel and the spiritual growth of readers. The body of Christ needs a variety of styles from Christian authors.

Paul was not speaking specifically of Christian writers,

but he was referring to believers involved in ministry when he wrote to the Corinthian church: "What ... is Apollos? And what is Paul? Only servants .... I planted the seed, Apollos watered it, but God made it grow. So neither he who plants nor he who waters is anything, but only God, who makes things grow. The man who plants and the man who waters have one purpose, and each will be rewarded according to his own labor. For we are God's fellow workers" (1 Corinthians 3:5-9).

Writing to change lives is not writing material that is, in and of itself, always life-changing. It is part of a process that will cause lives to be changed. Sometimes it begins a work; other times it continues or completes. Sometimes it even reinforces or reminds. All Christian writers do part of the work of ministry in each reader's life. Seek God for the niche He has for you.

I receive both critical and positive mail. One letter said, "Your column changed my life." This is clearly an overstatement, but something there built on what God was already doing and God used it. Think of what influence you can have. Someone God has been dealing with may read your writing. Some little thing you write may be the final piece in a mosaic of influences God has used in that reader's life.

Writing is a ministry partnership with coworkers who have or will touch those lives in different ways. The Christian writer's overall goal is to glorify Christ and build His kingdom. Ego should not be involved. Attitude is important. It should be one of service and humility. One of our writers hung a sign in his cubicle that said, "Servant's quarters." I like to see that in a writer.

To change lives, you will teach and inspire your readers. Here are some things you must do to change lives:

1. Your own life must have undergone significant change. Feed your spirit—and not just with things you can write about. A strong devotional life is indispensable for a Christian author.

2. Be personal and vulnerable. Some of the most effective articles are those in which the author admits a weakness that God helped him or her to conquer. You don't always need to supply an answer. Sometimes people just need to know there are others who struggle with the same issues they face and that there is hope.

3. Hit the readers where they are. Always ask, "Who are the readers and what are their needs?" Freelance writers often lose the focus of their audience. A seminary professor can't write on an academic level in a magazine for a general church audience, but needs to be able to write in a popular style. You may write for laypeople with all kinds of backgrounds, like the *Evangel's* readers—or you may write to a more specialized audience. This means two things:

• You don't need to tell everything you know.

• If you're not an expert, you may still have something to give. Sometimes writers who are not experts can bring freshness to their topic.

Find markets that fit your writing, rather than trying to make your writing fit a particular market.

4. Be convinced you are writing in God's will. Get God's direction both in a general and specific way.

5. Bathe your writing in prayer. Pray for anointing on the writing process. I usually pray with people I interview—and often have them pray for our staff. Pray for anointing on the finished work. Each week our staff lays hands on and prays for the next Sunday's issue. Pray with other writers, or those who will support your writing.

6. Set specific goals. What do you want this article/book to accomplish? "If you aim at nothing," someone has said, "you'll hit it every time." Do you want readers to ooh and ahh at your ability? Or do you want them to come away with something that will impact their lives?

As a pastor, I felt good when people said "Great message, Pastor." But I always felt better when I saw people's lives impacted.

7. Make sure you have a message. You can't change anyone's life if there is no substance. To have substance you don't need to "preach"—being "too preachy" is a common error in Christian circles. Your illustration may speak for itself. That's why our readers' favorite articles are stories about people. Such a story tells the reader something that happened in someone else's life, and the lesson learned. The reader can then apply it to his or her own experience.

8. Pinpoint one area to write about. If there is too much to focus on, readers may not remember anything. Find your core message—a task best fulfilled through seeking God's will and nurturing a regular prayer life—and stick to it. Careful editing of your writing will help you fulfill this goal. Cut the dead weight. Keep the life-giving central thoughts.

9. Give readers something memorable. The parts of sermons people remember most are (as much as we hate to admit it) humor, illustrations, mistakes—and stories about people. Don't just tell readers how; show them how with a true story.

10. Give people a reason to want to know more about your topic. Your writing may be the impetus for readers to seek out deeper truths. Life change may come through their subsequent search, instigated by your article.

11. Give up ownership of your work. You work belongs to God, first of all. You also give up a certain degree of control when you entrust your writing to a publisher. The finished product probably won't look exactly as you had it. God will still use it.

Here's an exercise that will help budding writers. Answer the following questions:

• How most would I like to change lives?

• How has my life been changed/impacted for the better? Is it worth writing about? Why/why not? How can I communicate this?

• What have I learned that changed my life? Is it worth writing about? Why/why not? How can I teach this?

Christian writing is not just a hobby or an occupation. It's ministry, and good writing changes lives.

7

Four Goals of Pentecostal Writing

By Randy Hurst

As a writer you should have each of four objectives guiding you regardless of your task at hand. These objectives may differ in proportion, but they should always influence your writing. Every writer should *inform, instruct, inspire* and *incite.*

Inform the reader.

To inform is to testify or share what God has done. Informative writing serves a purpose similar to a spoken testimony in a Pentecostal service. It lifts the faith of others.

The Assemblies of God's roots are tied to informative writing. In 1913, *Word and Witness*, a publication, called people to gather at Hot Springs, Ark., for a meeting that birthed the Fellowship. To help move the Fellowship forward, several publications merged, the *Pentecostal Evangel* was formed and the Assemblies of God began its history founded on a commitment to publish the works of God in people's lives.

Instruct the reader.

The only symbol on the Assemblies of God shield is a Bible. The first point in the Fellowship's foundational truths is an acknowledgment of the Bible's inspiration and infallibility. Our motto is "all the gospel."

The Christian writer should always try to convey biblical truth. This doesn't mean everything written is expositional. But it does mean that whatever is written will be biblically sound and will teach the reader in the process.

Simply reporting on events is not enough. Life lessons must be included. This need is greatest in educational materials. Sunday school quarterlies, for example, are far more instructional than a news report on a revival. But even when reporting on revival, the writer can in some way instruct the reader.

Inspire the reader.

Inspiration is not just affecting the reader emotionally. It is communicating Spirit-anointed concepts that will directly influence the reader's life.

Pentecostal writing shares not only timeless truth, but also timely truth. It takes the timeless lessons of God's Word and applies them directly to the critical issues of here and now. Pentecostal writers need to view writing as preaching and pray about what they put on paper. Writing is not just about transmitting ideas. It is a Spirit-driven compulsion to communicate truth the reader needs to hear.

Writers who inspire others must first be inspired themselves. Some try to write inspirational material based on an appeal to the reader's emotions. But the most inspiring is that which comes from the writer's own emotional makeup. If that emotional foundation is genuine, it will strike a chord in the reader.

This task also has a prophetic element. Think for a moment of the definition of a prophet. Simply, he or she is one who "speaks for God." It is not always *foretelling*—a message about what God will do in the *future*. It is most often *forth*telling—a message about what God deems important in the *here and now*. The Old Testament is filled with examples of prophets who carried God's truth to His people, and much of their work was through the written word. The New Testament expands on that picture with God's promise to pour out His Spirit on all believers so they can participate in conveying God's truth to a perishing world.

People need to be lifted spiritually. They need to be encouraged. They need to be exhorted. They need their faith strengthened. They need hope and peace. These needs are not met simply through conveying information. The Pentecostal writer must be both inspired and inspiring.

A good test of the inspiration factor is the written piece's effect on the writer. If what I'm writing does not move me, it probably won't move anyone else. The writer should not merely try to focus pragmatically on a predefined audience and write something that will appeal to them. The writer must first personally feel the impact of what he or she is writing.

Incite the reader.

To incite means the writer moves the reader to a decision. Most of the context in which I've written in recent years has been world missions. When writing concerning missions, I have three objectives, and all of them are directed toward an action by the reader. Writing concerning missions should move readers to *pray*. Without God's power, evidenced through our missionaries and their work, our mission will fail. And God acts in response to believing prayer. Missions writing also should move readers to *give* so that missionaries will have the necessary funds for their ministries. And it should move readers to *go* themselves into world missions.

I was blessed to learn that a youth pastor was reading an article I had written for the *Pentecostal Evangel* about the desperate spiritual needs of young people in Europe. That article confirmed God's call on his life, and he left his youth pastorate to enter missions.

My father-in-law, Gustav Bergstrom, planted churches in more than 250 cities in Brazil. As a young man, he read an article in the *Pentecostal Evangel* about Central Bible College and felt led to enroll there. A few years later, while pastoring, he sensed God's specific call to missions in Brazil while reading a magazine article about Latin America. Both of these major decisions in his life came about because of material he read.

By being obedient to the Holy Spirit's moving, writers will move others to act in obedience to the Spirit's call on their lives. It may not be about a specific ministry-related task, but it will call on readers to live holier lives, show compassion to those in need, deepen their commitment to God and fuel passion for reaching the spiritually lost.

Pentecostal writers essentially preach on paper. They

ask themselves: "What decision am I calling for in this article?" After reading the article, what will the reader's response be? Will they say, "I'm going to read my Bible every day" or "I'm going to get involved in feeding the hungry?" The writer should always move the reader to a decision—a decision compelled by biblical truth. To do anything else is a waste of paper.

8

The Mediocre Writer's Guide

By Randy Hurst

I'm basically a mediocre writer. I have to work hard at writing. I believe most writers feel the same way. Not even one Christian writer in a million will become the next C.S. Lewis. But every writer can learn basic principles from great writers and apply them.

Write short sentences.

Many writers have been helpful influences on my writing, but probably the two most significant were C.M. Ward and C.S. Lewis.

C.M. Ward was the longtime speaker for the Assemblies of God's *Revivaltime* radio broadcasts. I was in my teens and the Assemblies of God was holding a conference in Springfield, Mo., where I lived. Ward was speaking at a workshop on writing.

People think of Ward as a radio speaker. If you listened to his broadcasts, you'll remember that he crafted great sentences. I only remember one thing from the workshop, and it had to do with sentences. He said, "Write short sentences, verbs close to the front." That was my first lesson in writing.

Unfortunately, my sentences have grown like a fungus over the years. But I have never forgotten Ward's advice. I always try to shorten my sentences, and I almost always position verbs as close to the front as possible unless a qualifying or descriptive clause is especially significant to the primary thought of the sentence.

One of the things lacking in many people's writing is the finely crafted sentence. Acquiring this skill is a matter of discipline. Writers should try to get their meaning across as succinctly as possible and usually place the action early in the sentences so the reader knows what is happening.

Concerning composition, Samuel Johnson, author of the first English dictionary, stated: "Read over your compositions, and wherever you meet with a passage you think is particularly fine, strike it out!" The point is, when a sentence draws attention to its own beauty, it is distracting attention from the content. A sentence is a unit of thought, not a work of art. Sentences must not draw attention to their own construction, or they become an artifice instead of a medium. That's where I find a great editor to be invaluable.

Anyone who wants to be a great writer, or write to his or her greatest potential, cannot be paranoid of editors. Editors are writers' best friends. I want every editor I know and trust to read every article I write before publication. Editors help writers do better than their own best. Defensive and paranoid writers only do disservice to their own writing.

Pause for power.

Connected to the building block of the short sentence is the power of the pause. Most writers have failed to learn how to use short sentences to create necessary pauses. Eloquence is important, but the writer who can come up with a very brief sentence to insert among five long sentences will strengthen the entire paragraph. Contrast in writing is as vital as contrast in speaking. We talk about how boring a monotone can be, and we often equate a monotone with a soft or quiet voice. But someone who shouts out every sentence is also speaking in monotone. When someone writes at a fever pitch with long sentences and grandiose constructions, a literary monotone is the result. Just as the speaker alters the volume of voice and the pace of speech, the writer alters the length and energy of sentences in writing. All of the above is still summed up by Ward's adage, "Write short sentences, verbs close to the front."

Write to the ear.

In many ways, my all-time favorite writer is C.S. Lewis. Actually, I enjoy reading Lewis' letters even more than his books. Although Lewis never wrote a book about writing, he did respond to letters requesting advice concerning writing. The following observations were taken from his personal correspondence.

One of Lewis' simple yet profound teachings was, "Write to the ear." I try to, but I sometimes forget to read my material out loud before I submit it to an editor. Now the question might arise, "How many people really read out loud?" In reality, we all read out loud. We all have a mental narrator in our heads when we read, and that narrator reads with all the emotion and inflection we would use if reading aloud. Writers who read their material out loud to themselves will discover the little glitches that give readers pause. Reading out loud is a powerful self-editing tool that reveals words or clauses or sentences that sound awkward.

Don't ask your reader to do your work.

Another of Lewis' guidelines is tougher: "Don't ask your reader to do your work for you." For example, don't tell your reader that "it was a frightening night." Describe the night so that your reader is frightened. It is lazy writing to simply list what the intended emotion should be. Compelling writing creates the emotion you want your readers to feel.

You cannot inspire a reader unless you are inspired yourself. You have to read what you wrote and ask yourself what it does to you intellectually and emotionally. If it doesn't move you, it won't move anyone else. If it doesn't scare you, it won't scare anyone else. If it doesn't sadden you, it won't sadden anyone else.

All of the points made in this chapter are related in some way to restraint. In our excess-plagued society, the temptation is to be over-the-top in one's writing. Sometimes the writer's own ambitions get in the way of a powerful but simple message. The writer who is willing to discipline his or her craft and be true to the Spirit-inspired motives behind a particular piece will bring about long-term responses from readers rather than knee-jerk reactions.

Restraint in writing is similar to restraint in speaking or singing. A speaker who releases emotionally charged statements while keeping emotions in check has a powerful effect on an audience. A talented bass or soprano who refrains from singing the lowest or highest note in his or her range moves listeners far more deeply than singers who push their vocal limits.

A myth of writing is that you have to be a "natural" in order to do it. Natural abilities are a great help, of course. But every writer can become more effective if he or she will work hard and learn from others.

9

Effective Interviewing

By John W. Kennedy

I began in journalism by spending 11 years working at daily newspapers in Iowa and California, covering everything from the police to the religion beats. Afterwards I worked as associate news editor for *Christianity Today* for seven years before coming to the *Pentecostal Evangel* in 1999.

While the publications I've worked for have different purposes, there are some principles that apply to every reporter who conducts an interview. There are two basic elements to a story: gathering the information and then reporting it. Good writing doesn't just happen. It starts with solid interviews. And preparation is necessary for an interview to go well. You don't just start writing an article without giving it some thought. Likewise, you don't conduct an interview without a plan.

Whether talking in person or over the phone, a

reporter first needs to establish a level of trust. The best way to do that is to be friendly, personable, and enthusiastic. It's important to set your source at ease. Subjects whose experience with the media has been a negative one may be naturally suspicious or even hostile.

Set up the interview.

The guidelines I'm addressing are the lengthy interview, the one for a cover story or in-depth article.

When you begin your interview request, try to get to the top source, even in large organizations or ministries. Don't assume you can't gain an audience with the leader simply because he/she is a household name. Make sure the source knows what publication you represent and when the article is likely to appear. If you are part of a company or denomination that is different from the publication's name, mention it. While that may or may not open doors, at least the interviewee knows what you represent. Be clear about the purpose of the interview. Once you begin chatting with someone who thinks you are there to talk about her next singing tour, when in fact you want to focus on how to stay pure while a celebrity, you're in trouble.

Set up an interview time that is convenient to the source. You want to be accommodating, because the source is usually doing you a favor by giving up a part of the day to provide information you couldn't obtain otherwise.

Make sure the person knows up front that you want to go on the record and use quotes. You don't want to be talking for an hour and then hear the subject say, "You can't use my name." Before the questioning begins, ascertain whether there is anything potentially controversial that needs to be off the record. Some people are legitimately fearful of reprisals.

Pick the right location.

Interviewing in person is best because you can see the subject in a natural work or family environment. What does he have on his desk? How does she interact with her staff? What facial expressions and mannerisms does he use when answering your questions? These all can be incorporated as colorful elements of the story.

But you may not want to let the person be too comfortable. If the interviewee is surrounded by co-workers while you're asking for details, she may not open up as much as she would if no others were listening.

Some reporters and sources prefer a neutral location, such as a restaurant. If you do go to an eatery, make sure you don't order too much to eat. It's difficult to concentrate on asking questions, taking notes and munching on cuisine at the same time. In addition, be aware that restaurants—and many public places—are noisy. Too many reporters have discovered this while trying to transcribe a tape recording of the conversation later. If you are in a restaurant, try to be seated at a table where the subject has a view of the corner. The fewer visual distractions, the better the answers.

Should you use a recorder?

Tape recorders are a good idea if they are used to supplement your notes. It's always wise to have a cassette tape as a backup to check for accuracy—especially if that source is difficult to reach or is someone of prominence.

Still, you need to be a reliable note-taker and to develop some system of shorthand even when you are using a tape. If you are recording, go ahead and write notes as though you were not. Cassettes and recorders have a knack for failing.

Before the interview begins, ask the person's permission to record. Although most people have no problem with taping, don't assume that it's OK. Tape recorders make some sources nervous. In the mind of some people, a tape recorder means you are an antagonist trying to trick them into divulging information. Occasionally a source will turn the tables and plop down his own tape recorder, which can indeed be intimidating. But recording devices shouldn't be a threat. Set subjects at ease by explaining you just want to get the details right.

Make sure you have enough tapes and working batteries before you arrive. The appearance of a bumbling reporter doesn't make for a smooth start.

Do your homework.

Once you begin the interview, don't open with a remark that shows your lack of preparation. If the first impression by your source is that you have done little groundwork, it can quickly shut down an interviewee's receptivity to answering further questions. If the source senses that you are a lightweight, he's likely to give curt answers while he's planning the rest of his day in his mind.

As the interview progresses, the inquiries should become tougher. Your inquiries should require more than a "yes" or "no" response. The why and how questions demand the most thought. In addition, open-ended questions oblige a subject to contemplate an answer rather than merely recite a response given many times before.

If you are writing an article about a Christian leader, you should know beforehand how she got started, where she lives, if she is married. Look over books and articles that person has written. Look at the organization's Web site for a biography of the subject and a fact sheet about the ministry.

Research your subject independently. Be a voracious reader of newspapers, magazines, books and Internet sites for background information. Keep in mind that opinions posted on the Internet may not be accurate or fair.

Use the information you have gathered as background to guide you during the conversation. Research is no substitute for comments made in your direct interview. Most of the information that ends up in your article likely will come from talking to the person yourself.

Prepare questions in advance.

A successful interview depends not only on how willing your source is to talk, but also on how you phrase the questions. I suggest writing out questions in advance. I jot, in light pencil, the gist of the question staggered down the left margin of a notepad. Don't read the questions off the notebook, but work them into the conversation naturally. For later reference, I always put down details at the top of the page such as when the interview was set up and the date it was conducted.

If you've established a good rapport early, the source should be at ease at the end even though the subject matter is more intense. Keep the questions brief. The more detailed and rambling a question is, the more convoluted the answer.

You can miss a much better story if you fail to ask the right questions, or if you ask the questions in the wrong way. If you pose simplistic questions, you'll likely receive vague responses.

Start the interview right.

In the interview you need to try to establish an instant bond. Because you may have only 15 minutes with your subject, it's essential to get off on the right foot. Once you've exchanged greetings, quickly remind the source who you are, what publication you represent and the purpose of the story. Some people have several interviews a week, so don't presume they are eagerly awaiting your arrival. After reviewing your reason for being there, engage in some friendly but brief chitchat. You might comment about an interesting fact you learned in research, such as "You're originally from southeast Iowa, too." Or, noting the family photo on the desk, say, "I have three sons as well."

But don't become so wrapped up in divulging your family history that you eat up precious time. Most people who are interesting enough to become a major feature article are busy, so use the allotted minutes wisely.

You cannot control all the variables. Your interview may be a disaster because the source had an argument with his wife just before talking to you. Or he may be in physical pain. If the subject obviously isn't up to answering questions, you may want to try at a later date, if his schedule and your deadline allow.

Be courteous during the interview.

Keep in mind some lessons from childhood: show good manners, be genuine, dress appropriately, speak distinctly. In most opinion polls, journalists rank near used car salesmen and politicians in the trust department.

In certain situations you need to show Christlike sympathy rather than hard-nosed interrogation. I once had to interview a woman whose brother, niece and nephew had been killed in an arson fire the night before. Initially, the situation called for me to express sorrow and allow her to express her emotions rather than answer questions. This wasn't a time to hurry back to the office.

Be polite, yet businesslike. Don't fawn over the source by saying something like, "I'm totally in awe of your ministry." Keep your readers in mind. Are they going to learn as much if you are writing to please the source rather than inform your audience?

Keep eye contact, nod, smile, respond verbally with phrases such as "Is that right?" or "Really?" By showing an interest you likely will receive better information.

As a reporter you are there to gather information, not to spout your opinions. Recently I conducted a phone interview of a father whose son had been executed. During the conversation he told me he didn't believe in the "goofy notion of hell." While I disagreed with his outlook, my role was to focus on the topic at hand, so I guided the discussion back to capital punishment.

If I had pursued a theological tangent I might have

scored some debate points but I would have missed the purpose of the interview: to talk about his views on his son being put to death. If you are talking to someone whose religious beliefs are vastly different, you need to show professional courtesy rather than contempt.

Ask for explanation.

Don't be embarrassed to ask for a clarification or restatement during the interview if you really don't follow what the person is talking about. If she starts talking at length about someone you haven't heard of, you better find out more before plunging deeper into uncharted waters. It may be humiliating, but it's better than losing your train of thought and writing down wrong information. When an interviewee is talking above your head, say, "Would you explain that some more?" or "Could you provide an example?"

When you interject this way, it also can buy some time in catching up on your note-taking. Don't be afraid to say, "Could you repeat that again a little slower?"

Don't miss the real story.

Always be observing details. Is there something unusual about this person's mannerisms or speech? Think a step ahead of where you want the interview to go, what the next question should be. If the subject brings up a topic that sparks another question, jot it down in the margin so you don't forget to pursue it.

Prepared questions are simply a guide to get started. Be ready to depart from your fixed game plan if the answers take you in a startling direction. Spontaneous follow-up questions sometimes result in the liveliest material. But don't get sidetracked by a source who tries to take the interview down a different path from the one you need.

A danger of being tied to a list of questions is that you fail to pick up on what unanticipated additional details are offered. If the subject drops a bombshell, it's time to rechart your course.

Don't be so preoccupied with getting your questions in that you miss what important particulars the person is saying at the moment. By gaining trust and asking intelligent questions, you may embolden the source to reveal information he hasn't felt comfortable disclosing to other reporters. It's important to find an angle that hasn't been reported before, especially for subjects who wind up on the cover of multiple magazines.

Follow-up questions arise from an unexpected response. If she raises a topic that explores interesting new territory, you need to be quick to pick up on it. A startling response such as "There is no hope for America" begs for more of an explanation and could very well become the lead of your story.

Leave the door open.

Thank the source at the end of the interview, but don't close your mind. Sometimes some of the best nuggets come after you get out of your chair, turn off the tape recorder and are walking toward the door. Don't be afraid to ask if you can take down an additional statement.

Try to obtain all the information you need at the interview, but don't feel awkward if you need to call back and check details: the date on which something occurred; the exact details of a lengthy story; the spelling of names. Never assume spellings.

The guidelines in this chapter may not work for every situation in every publication. But I encourage you to continually be honing your skills, learning from past mistakes and using what techniques work best for your situation.

10

Slants and Angles

By John W. Kennedy

Several major differences between news reporting and feature writing are in style and presentation. News articles tend to be shorter, more to the point and packed with information. In Christian circles, a journalist must be truthful to biblical principles but also wary that churchgoers don't always see eye to eye.

Timeliness is also a factor. Few Christian publications have a next-week turnaround. A two-month delay is common from the time the manuscript is submitted to when it is printed. And in this day of around-the-clock news networks and Internet communications, a hard news story really isn't likely to be hot by the time it appears in an evangelical publication.

So if the topic you are covering, say an American missionary murdered by an Asian rebel group, already has been reported at length in the secular press, you need to find a different approach.

By the time most Christian publications reported the September 11 terrorist attacks in November, they had to find an angle beyond thousands who died when hijacked jets rammed into the Twin Towers, the Pentagon and a field in Pennsylvania. Enterprising Christians had little trouble finding stories within the larger event: How did faith help those who escaped death that day? What role did the clergy play in meeting the needs of the injured and those who lost loved ones? How did Christian agencies respond to the crisis?

Similar faith-based focuses can be the basis for national stories of lesser magnitude. Christian publications can fill a niche if they report on trends rather than hard news. Topics that *Today's Pentecostal Evangel* has covered lately in lengthy news articles include foster care, reality-based TV shows, Internet romances, credit card debt, illegal drugs and sexual predators. Christians approach such matters with a worldview that is far removed from the rest of society.

Structure the story.

The story lead should contain compelling information that will make the reader go to the second paragraph and beyond. Many other activities, not the least of which is television, compete for the attention of readers.

Many methods can be used to coax readers into an article. Leads used often in news include the immediate identification lead, which lists a well-known name, and the summary lead, which contains several important elements of the content that is about to follow.

More and more news writers are using feature-type

introductions in an effort to attract readers. This narrative or anecdotal lead can work well to explain a complex issue through the eyes of an individual. This is best primarily in longer articles where you want to paint a picture that appeals to the senses. But narrative leads can become trite and formulaic if overused. And if the article is short, such introductions are impractical.

Several leads don't work well in news. One is the introduction that is a quote from one of the subjects in the article. Rarely is a thought so well articulated that it captures the essence of what the story is about. Another weak lead is the question lead, such as, "Why are fewer people going to church today?" Readers want answers, not questions. Finally there is the "duh" lead, such as "Men are different from women." Why would anyone want to continue?

After the opening paragraph, use the second paragraph to convey different information that's not quite important enough to be part of the lead.

Sometimes the third or fourth paragraph serves as a nut graph, spelling out to the reader exactly what the story will deliver and why it is an important article to read.

In writing in the inverted pyramid style, you continue to introduce new information in descending order of importance, elaborating as you go. Use transitions to move the reader from one idea to the next.

Short, simple sentences convey conflict and action. Long sentences slow down the reader into a calmer frame of mind. Good stories should have sentences of varying lengths.

What's the point?

Make sure you understand the key elements of a story before you write. What is the primary theme that ties it all together? If you can't determine the focus, maybe there should be no story.

Writers shouldn't automatically include the date something happened in the first sentence if it makes your publication look slow in reporting it. If you are writing about a conference or meeting, lead with the most important outcome of the gathering, not a chronological recap of the event. Especially with stories that happen year after year you need a fresh approach.

For example, when I worked at *Christianity Today* one of the yearly events I covered was the National Religious Broadcasters (NRB) convention. My first year the following could have been the lead: "More than 4,000 delegates attended the 50th annual convention January 30 through February 1 in Washington, D.C." That's factual, but it's not compelling.

Instead someone not even in attendance became the lead: "After a dozen chummy years with the Reagan and Bush administrations, the National Religious Broadcasters this year for the first time declined to invite the president of the United States to address its annual convention."

Be specific.

When you are writing, explain exactly what you mean. A phrase such as "litigation might be pending" is ambiguous. Will a suit be filed next week or is the source just blowing smoke?

Don't fall into Christianese with terms such as "came to the Lord" or "prayed the sinner's prayer." While Christians may know what you're talking about, non-Christians won't understand.

The church started a number of years ago; several hundred attended the crusade; dozens died in the plane crash. All these approximate numbers could easily be converted into exact figures with a little more legwork. You don't need to go overboard on details if it has little bearing on the main theme. "Jones became a Christian in the 6 p.m. Sunday service, October 3, 1970." The year alone should suffice.

Don't assume that the reader knows complex theories of medicine or theology. A sentence of explanation in lay terms likely is needed.

Write clearly and concisely.

If you are writing for a general audience, use jargon that is understandable, not lofty, esoteric language. Get to the point quickly. *Said* is more to the point than *made the statement that. Although* is a good word to use in place of *despite the fact that. Now* is a better term than *at this point in time.*

In short news articles there's no need to be fancy. *Says* throughout a story is usually preferable to *stated, declared, exclaimed, announced, maintained, contended, claimed* or *added.* Those words often aren't entirely accurate.

Don't make the reader labor through a sentence opening replete with commas. "John Johnson, 45, senior pastor, First Assembly of God, Sacramento," makes the reader pause repeatedly. Although longer, an easier read is: "John Johnson, the 45-year-old senior pastor at

First Assembly of God in Sacramento."

Another turnoff is passive construction rather than the active voice. A story with sentences full of "was" and "were" usually is a result of lazy writing. Here's an example: "The trip was coordinated by King's Castle and participants were required to participate in evangelism training." Turning it around makes it better: "King's Castle coordinated the trip in which participants received evangelism training."

Don't jump to conclusions: "The conference inspired and refreshed the 30,000 men in attendance." There's no way to know that.

Think carefully before applying a label to an individual or organization. Pro-choice. Heathen. Right-winger. Radical. All are strong identifiers that often are misapplied.

Do the reporting yourself. I've had writers turn in stories with direct quotes cited in the *Wall Street Journal*, *Newsweek* and CNN. If a story is worth running, a reporter should be able to track down sources rather than quote other publications. I've also had writers who steal copy from published sources without attribution. That's plagiarism and it's bad.

Keep your focus in mind.

There is such a thing as overreporting. I remember a cub reporter who wrote his first 1,500-word lead news article. He didn't want to miss anything. One source led him to another source who led him to another source. He ended up interviewing 60 people. That's too many. Unless you are writing an investigative piece and need background, there shouldn't be a reason to spend hours on the phone talking to people who won't make it into a story. How many people are enough to interview? It depends on the length and complexity of the piece. But it should be obvious when a pattern is established. If four sources are giving you pretty much the same information, you probably can begin writing. But if four people are feeding you thoroughly diverse material, more probing may be in order. Generally the broader perspective you have, the more well-rounded story results. It is better to have too much information than not enough.

For major pieces I may interview 10 people, but only five might make it into print.

If a source leads you to a new angle, that may become a new section of the article or another story altogether.

Tell differing viewpoints.

A bigger problem is underreporting, especially one-source stories that miss the mark. There is more than one way Christians view issues such as hunger, school prayer, homelessness and capital punishment. While your publication may advocate a particular stance, you should at least include the mention of the other side. Otherwise it becomes an editorial.

In the before-mentioned NRB story, *CT* reached the president, who said he would have attended the convention if invited.

Just as in the movies, tension is an important element in news stories. More and more that conflict is biblical Christianity versus an increasingly vocal secular society that sees nothing wrong with behaviors that nearly everyone used to find sinful. The strife is evident in areas such as abortion, homosexuality, gambling and pornography.

Don't create tension that's not there. For instance, if two agencies have different methods to help the homeless it doesn't necessarily mean they are at odds.

You should not use a story as a bully pulpit for strong viewpoints you possess. There is a fine line between analysis and opinion. A careful writer can convey conflict in subtle ways without sermonizing or appearing judgmental. Allow sources to speak as authority figures rather than you as a writer conveying the same thoughts. There is a journalistic and biblical way to be objective and evangelical. A news story is not the place for the writer to get on a soapbox to advocate a viewpoint.

Objectivity also involves full disclosure. If you are on the board or employed in some capacity for an organization, you shouldn't be pitching freelance article ideas about the group to an unsuspecting publication.

Make smooth transitions.

Transitions are like road signs. They tell the reader that a new section is ahead. It may simply be a phrase such as "on the other hand" or just a word such as "however."

If you can't easily determine where you are going in the story, readers definitely won't be able to follow the course. An article shouldn't meander from thought to thought without supporting evidence.

A story should have a definite stopping point rather than ending abruptly right after introducing a new idea. The ending may tie back to the lead, summarize the points of the story in a restated fashion or raise the question of what will happen in the future. It may be best to give the last word to the main source, especially if that person is driving home a point that is a repeated theme. Don't give the last word to a speaker whose views are opposite of the magazine's mission.

Make quotes worthwhile.

Quotes should be confined to the following: when a source says something unusual; says something in an unusual way; says something in a manner that gets the point across strongly; or says something significant.

Many quotes that appear in manuscripts are better paraphrased. Too many writers submit stories that for the most part are a string of quotes interrupted only occasionally by a transitional sentence. That's not reporting.

In making every word of a story count, one of the best places to trim is quotes. Writers don't need to set up quotes with a sentence that says virtually the same particulars. Here is such an example:

> Smith says the ministry's philosophy of reaching men for Christ has not changed. "Our philosophy of reaching men for Christ is the same as it's always been," Smith says.

In this case it really isn't helpful because "reaching men for Christ" is vague.

Extra verbiage such as *I really believe, in my opinion* and *I think* should be excised. So should overused words like *very* and misused words such as *hopefully*. Eliminate one of the redundant words in pairings such as *future goals, central emphasis* and *true fact*.

A quote from a state highway transportation official recently in a local newspaper about widening a stretch of highway violated several of these writing rules:

"This is probably, in my estimation, one of the more

unique projects."

Factual details don't need to be part of a quote. "The church began meeting in a living room five years ago and now has more than 5,000 members."

It's better to paraphrase if the thoughts conveyed in a quote are unclear. Usually quotes longer than two successive sentences bog down the reader.

Double-check everything.

Even after the story is written, take the time to make that extra phone call to find out the answer to the question that has been nagging you in the back of your mind. Is there someone you should have interviewed that you neglected?

Double-check the spelling of names, ages, syntax, grammar and attribution before filing. It's best to let the story marinate overnight and proofread it again before filing rather than sending it off immediately.

Question statistics. Don't repeat figures that have made the rounds on e-mail without much research. Examples include the percentage of Christians who are divorced, how many Christians were martyred in the 20th century and what percentage of Americans are Christians.

If you fail on spellings and figures the rest of your reporting is suspect.

11

Three Lessons I Paid $25,000 to Learn

By Kirk Noonan

I like to stretch my dollars as far as they will go. One of the best ways to do that, I have learned, is to share.

Following are three of the most important lessons I learned while in graduate school. The cost for me to learn these lessons was $25,000. The cost for you is simply the price of this book.

Lesson 1: What do you love?

Bob Slosser swaggered into the classroom and tossed his briefcase on the desk. He didn't say a word, but the bravado that followed him through the door screamed, "I'm in charge." After digging through his briefcase he pulled out a class list and called our names alphabetically. Slosser noted who was present then slid right into what he had to say.

"If this were a ladder," he said, using his index finger to draw an imaginary ladder, "and we were talking about your writing skills, you would be here."

He pointed to what would be the lowest rung on the ladder.

"It's my job to help you reach the top rung of the ladder," he continued, pointing his finger toward the ceiling. "But if you're not serious about becoming a better writer, then leave now. We don't need you."

I already respected Slosser. Before class started I had learned he used to be an editor at the *New York Times*. But now, after only a few minutes in his presence, I also feared him.

"There are many things you're going to learn in this class," he continued. "Perhaps the most important thing you're going to discover is whether you're in love with writing or the thought of being a writer."

I sat up straight in my seat. My mind raced and I questioned my motives for uprooting my family and moving across the country to attend graduate school so that I could chase my dream of becoming a writer.

Did I really love writing, or did I just love the idea of being a writer?

Slosser's question weighed heavily on my mind. I grappled with it throughout that first semester in his class as he tore virtually every story I wrote to shreds with his red pen.

Even today his question resurfaces, especially when I am up against a tight deadline or wading through pages of research or mining a long interview looking for just the right quote. Sometimes the question haunts me when I receive a nasty letter or an angry phone call from a reader who did not like one of my articles. A demanding editor's criticism can force the question from its hiding place in my mind.

When I come up against adversities writers face daily the only thing that keeps me coming back for more is my answer to the question.

Yes, I love writing more than I love the idea of being a writer.

Do you?

If you do, keep writing.

If you don't, find something else to do. To be a good writer you're going to have to have something more pushing you than a desire to be something you're not.

Lesson 2: Take the reader there.

The blacktop road ends in Makuyuni. In a wink we pass the tiny town's gas station, restaurant and motel before veering onto a rutted dirt road. Like jet-trails, dust clouds billow from our Toyota Land Cruiser's back wheels. Inside, we brace ourselves with every bone-jarring hole and bump the SUV's suspension does not absorb.

"It's at least seven hours from here depending on the roads," says Scott Hanson, our host, interpreter, driver and guide. "In Tanzania we don't judge travel by how many kilometers away something is; we judge it by how many hours it takes to get there."

Already we are an hour behind schedule thanks to a mishap in Arusha, a growing city near the Kenyan border where our journey began. While getting supplies, a friend of Hanson's who we are taking to a village accidentally locked the keys in the truck. After an hour, two local men were able to get into the truck and we were on our way. But now Hanson is worried that we might not make it to Wasso, our destination, before nightfall. "We're going to have to push it," Hanson says. "Bandits and bad roads make it very dangerous for us to be caught in the bush at night."

In the village of Mto Wa Mbu we bid Hanson's friend farewell and buy bananas from street vendors who swarm around the Land Cruiser. Marketing here is simple: throw bananas through open Land Cruiser window and tourists will feel obligated to buy. We do and are happy with our purchase because the bananas are delicious. Unknown to us they are also one of the last luxuries we will have for the next five days ....

When I wrote this scene my goal was simple: I wanted the reader to feel as though he were in Tanzania going on safari. Part of my job at *Today's Pentecostal Evangel* is to travel to other countries and report on the work of missionaries. Taking readers to a country unfamiliar to them and introducing them to a people and culture through my writings is one of the highlights of my job. For me, that is what the "take the reader there" concept is all about.

Following are some simple guidelines I follow when I am collecting information about the scene I am going to be setting:

• Read as many books, travel brochures, maps, Web sites and magazines about the place to be visited as possible.

• While on-site rely on all senses.

• Look for unique details.

• Take copious notes.

• Ask as many questions of sources as possible.

• Carry a camera and take pictures.

To be good at taking the reader there you don't have to be a great writer; you just have to be a good story-

teller. Once you have collected all your information
you're ready to write. Here are my rules:

- Write the story like I would tell it.
- Include the details I worked so hard to get.
- Keep it simple.
- Don't overuse adjectives.
- Rewrite until I'm more than satisfied.

When you are successful at taking your readers with
you, they will feel as though they have taken a journey.
But you'll have done more for them than just given
them a vacation from the rigors of life. You'll have
expanded their worldview and maybe even made them
think about a land, people, culture or issue they have
never considered before.

Lesson 3: Read, analyze and dissect.

A man once told me that originality is merely the art
of deception. I took that phrase and applied it to my
pursuit of becoming a writer. Am I advocating plagiarism? No way. But one of the best ways to become a
better writer is to read, analyze and dissect other people's work.

Pick up a magazine and pick out a story. Read it in
its entirety. Then comb over it looking for interesting
word combinations, phrases and styles that interest
you.

With pen in hand, begin dissecting the story. The first
thing to look at is the lead. Did it grab your attention
and force you to the next paragraph? If so, how did the
writer accomplish that?

The second thing you might look at is the nut graph,
which is a summary or thesis of what the piece is all
about. It is usually found near the beginning of the

article and serves as an anchor for the story. When you find it, ask yourself if the writer has clearly defined what you (the reader) will be getting yourself into.

Use a highlighter to mark phrases and words that appeal to you. Did the writer use a word in a way that is intriguing? Are there any phrases that play on a theme?

Also pay attention to the quotes. Does the person quoted sound natural or contrived? Is the quote worthy of even being a quote? Does the quote move the story forward? Is it set up adequately and supported well?

As you dissect the piece write notes in the margin. Draw conclusions on why you think the writer did what she did. Did she leave anything out? Could the story have been better? If so, how?

Combing over other people's work, especially those people who are being paid to write, can dramatically improve your writing and give you ideas when you sit down to write.

Pull it together.

Three lessons—I'm still learning them—as well as a host of others. But those three are a solid foundation for everything I write. If you approach your writing with an attitude of commitment, with a goal of transporting your readers and with a willingness to learn from other writers, you'll find yourself climbing that elusive ladder of talent.

12

Shave It, Cut It, Trim It—Just Make It Shorter

By Kirk Noonan

If you ever hiked a few miles to a campsite you know it's best to bring only what you need. Instead of packing a heavy iron pot, television/DVD combo, curling iron and mattress you're more likely to bring a lightweight collapsible pan, book, comb and sleeping bag. The same principle holds true for writing: bring what you need, not what you want.

Every editor I have worked for has lived by the same mantra: Make everything in your story count. If a paragraph, sentence or word is not needed, say "adios" to it no matter what. You'll deliver a tighter, sharper, better story to your reader and he or she might thank you by reading your entire piece.

The problem with most of us writers is that we can't imagine a world where less is more. But readers' attention spans are short and they aren't willing to wade through drivel. So, make all your writings concise.

Give it what it's worth.

Many young writers, and even some older ones, believe that including every bit of minutia on a subject means a job well done. Wrong! Good writers only give their readers pertinent and needed information.

When I started working at *Today's Pentecostal Evangel* I reported to a young editor named Joel Kilpatrick. My first months on the job, Kilpatrick read over every story I wrote. Each day he would return to my desk with one of my stories in hand.

"Trim to 300 or below," he'd say flatly. "It doesn't deserve any more than that."

What am I supposed to do with the other 650 words? I'd wonder as he slinked back to his office.

After getting over the shock of Kilpatrick's appraisal I started trimming one word at a time. Sometimes, it felt like killing a friend as I lopped off sentences that seemed to sing. Inevitably, as I studied the piece, combined ideas and chopped words and quotes, I realized Kilpatrick was right. Much of the article was fluff.

Many of us pack our stories with fluff for self-serving reasons. I used to overwrite so my editors would see how much reporting I had done. But good reporting doesn't matter if people don't read your article.

It usually took an hour or so to cut my stories to Kilpatrick's 300-word maximum. But on every occasion the end result was worth the effort. The improvement was obvious in the sleeker version. Rather than just a sentence or two singing, the entire piece harmonized like a 500-member choir.

Good writers are good editors.

Good editors scrutinize every word, sentence, phrase and paragraph. They swarm over other people's work looking for flaws in logic, grammar and style. An editor's work may go unrecognized but it serves a vital function in clarifying your content.

Writers need to become good self-editors to take their writing to the next level. Learn to write short yet compelling and complete material. With each idea, ask yourself a simple question: Who cares?

Who cares? should be your judge and jury when it comes to any piece of information.

• Will anyone benefit from the information?

• Will the information move the story forward?

• Is the information cogent and relative to your main point?

• Can the story be as effective or even more effective without the information?

Put quotations to the *Who Cares?* test as well. If your subjects don't say something original or enlightening, don't quote them. You will only make people look boring and reveal the weakness of your questions.

Testing everything in your article will not necessarily shorten it. But what you put in your article, regardless of the word count, will be valuable information that has been put to the test.

Let it sit.

After you have finished your article abandon it. After a few days have passed, attack it again. Chop more if needed then read it out loud. How does it flow? Are the transitions smooth? Does it evoke emotion where it should? Did you convey all you intended?

Once you are satisfied, have other people read it. Let them tell you what they think. Ask questions of them that will improve the story. Remain open-minded to their suggestions even if you don't agree with them.

I let two friends read this piece before I turned it in. Unfortunately, I didn't follow my own rules. As soon as I finished it I sent it out. Combined, they found hundreds of words to chop. Ouch. Constructive criticism can hurt. But their input has made this a better piece.

What about my style?

Some writers feel threatened by writing concisely because they believe doing so will eliminate or affect their style. Don't worry. If anything, your style will improve as you create a solid piece free of frivolous facts, extra words and boring quotes.

With the piece at its essence you can add your touches. Keep in mind that adding style is done with sleight of hand. Don't overhaul the piece—that should already be done. Instead, tweak a few words and phrases so they pop off the page. At this stage you function more as an interior designer than a general contractor.

Throw in some color and accents. Make the piece distinct and alluring. But don't overdo it. Style can overshadow the story when it should only serve to highlight and add life.

Don't be afraid of the chopping block.

It's hard to chop your story into submission. But it is also one of the most rewarding tasks because you are making your piece attractive and more readable. As you sit down to write, remember: Less is more, and in most instances, more powerful, too.

13

Write Like You Talk

By Scott Harrup

"The Irish don't really think about writing," quipped best-selling Irish author Maeve Binchy in an editorial for the *New York Times*, "it is just a natural extension of what we do all the time, which is talking."

Talking and writing are inextricably linked. But for many people, writing is an intimidating task perceived to be on some higher plane than speaking. They feel overwhelmed by the process of writing out thoughts they might quickly and comfortably share in a conversation. If you fit into this camp, overcoming this barrier can be the means to releasing your creativity and easing your anxiety.

Writers type their sentences with the same words they use in speech. The real difference between writing and speaking is one of preparation, and this is both a blessing and a curse. What a person says hangs in the air unadorned for immediate judgment by the hearer.

This can give rise to misunderstanding, but for the most part the result is quick and effective communication. On the other hand, what a person writes can remain privately printed or stored on a hard drive through numerous revisions. No one has to see a single word until the entire piece has been polished. This can lead to highly accurate communication, but can also delay a needed message unnecessarily. The challenge for the writer is to find the balance between releasing a piece too early with avoidable mistakes and agonizing over the editing process to the point of grinding creativity to a halt.

It's inspiring to realize that God used writing as His primary tool for communicating with humanity. The Bible, the world's greatest book, includes the divinely orchestrated contributions of dozens of writers. But stop and think about what the Bible contains. So many of its verses directly or indirectly quote things that people said. When Jesus ministered on earth, He didn't write out sermons and have the disciples copy them for distribution. He spoke parables in everyday language, and those sayings became the backbone of the written Gospels. Paul's writings to the early churches come across as wise advice from a loving friend. When Paul is quoted, many of his statements sound conversational, thanks to his personal focus on his readers. He didn't set out to write books. Under the Holy Spirit's inspiration, he couched Christian theology in the everyday language of a letter.

When you remind yourself of the cooperative relationship between speech and writing, you take a giant step forward in your ability to put your thoughts onto paper. The following points will help you use the strengths of your spoken words to improve your written words. Along the way, we'll consider some weaknesses you can avoid.

Description

Think of an anecdote you would tell your best friend. You would look for words that conveyed a sense of time and place, so your friend could mentally go there with you. You would include relevant statements from other people involved in the story so your friend could hear the important things that were said. And you would direct all of the details of your story toward a concluding idea so your friend would understand the story's significance.

What you share might be as simple as an activity you pursued over the weekend. It might be something as complex as your views on the meaning of life. In either instance, how would you share that story? If you think of the story in terms of how you speak, you would convey it simply and economically. You would probably get the details across in just a few minutes in most cases, even if you ended up discussing the implications of that anecdote for another hour.

Take that economical approach to your writing. Look for ways to succinctly describe setting (time and place), dialog (relevant statements of other people) and theme (concluding or central idea). Jump-start your writing by imagining how you might tell your story in the least amount of time.

Writers can get bogged down with description. Speakers don't tend to make that mistake as easily. A speaker will matter-of-factly say that she mowed the lawn on Saturday. A writer is tempted to dwell on the sinuous blades of grass struggling upward through the loam to accept the sun's gift of nourishment completely heedless of the approaching roar of mechanized pruning ... you get the picture.

Once you have in place the bare bones of what you want to describe, you can fill in some helpful details. Just don't go overboard.

Emotion

The emotion in your writing is strongly tied to your description and, as in description, most of the time you will discover that less is more when it comes to conveying emotion. You and your friend talk about countless subjects covering topics that elicit laughter, sympathy, outrage and fear. But how often do you actually have to say to your friend, "This is really funny ... sad ... frightening"? You rely on your ability to describe what happened to make the emotional implications obvious. If your 2-year-old's latest potty-training escapade is hilarious, you will describe it in such a way as to earn a laugh or two. If your relative is dying of cancer, you will talk about that in an appropriate manner and no one will have to second-guess what kind of reaction you're looking for.

As you write, allow the clarity of your descriptions to move your reader toward the intended emotional response. Don't use punctuation (!!!), type style (the accident was *really* tragic), or unnecessary adjectives and adverbs (the tall, tanned, muscular, well-dressed man laughed uproariously) to hold up your writing. Ask yourself how you would tell a funny or sad story, then write out the basic details of that story that make it funny or sad. Again, during revision, you can fill in additional details. If you have laid out the framework clearly enough, your reader will already be headed toward the correct emotional response.

Conviction

The idea here is not to convict your reader in the sense of creating a guilt trip, but rather to share your belief in the importance of your message. Talking with your friend, you communicate the depth of your conviction through tone of voice and body language as well as word choice. Writing, you will be limited to word choice. But there are still ways to let your reader know that you are sharing important life truths.

If you're writing an essay, editorial or other nonfiction piece, you can utilize a first-person voice to bluntly state, "I believe ..." "I'm convinced that ..." "I've discovered that ...." Again, balance is needed. If every sentence begins with such a statement, your arguments will end up being weakened. For the most part, state facts as facts without qualification.

Personal conviction can empower your writing. Before you dive into a project, ask yourself some basic questions. Why is the subject important to me? How has my view on the subject affected my life? What impact will it have on my reader's life?

For the Christian writer, this line of questioning plays a vital role in sharing your testimony. You might not be writing an article that specifically outlines the plan of salvation; but, if you want to get across any kind of spiritual truth, it is vital that you be perceived as completely sold out to your point of view. Anemic evangelism is self-defeating.

Expression

You can probably name some people you admire for their ability to communicate verbally. They never seem to be at a loss for words, and they know how to get a point across clearly and completely. You can develop the same skills in your writing, and here is where writing can greatly expand your communication skills even beyond your ability to carry on a conversation. It doesn't matter if you are petrified of standing up and speaking in public, you can retreat to your favorite writer's nook and hammer out your thoughts with depth and style. All you have to do is be willing to rely on the right tools.

A dictionary, a thesaurus, a book on grammar—these are the basics. In an age of personal computers, all of these tools are available digitally, and their powers are dramatically increased. Do yourself a favor and purchase recognized classics in each field.

Have these tools nearby when you're writing. Don't just use them to check spelling, but take advantage of their ability to expand your vocabulary and enrich your sentences. A word of caution—the idea here is not to create a false academic atmosphere. You never want to come across as talking down to your reader. Your goal is to get across the greatest wealth of ideas in the most efficient manner possible.

Finally, look for opportunities to expand your writing vocabulary during your free time. Cast a critical eye on the books you read, even your light reading. You can learn a lot from your favorite authors. Crossword puzzles are another tool for building your word power while you relax.

Inspiration

"Let the words of my mouth, and the meditation of my heart, be acceptable in thy sight, O Lord, my strength, and my redeemer" (Psalm 19:14). As you learn to transition smoothly from speaking to writing, you're sure to notice an increase in your written output. But this connection brings up the vital importance of purifying your thoughts and words before you sit down to write in the first place.

Learning to write like you talk will only be a blessing if how you talk and who you talk to are above reproach. Communicate courteously and lovingly with those around you. You will energize your writing. Build deep relationships with other believers. You will energize your writing. Look for opportunities every day to talk to God in prayer. You will energize your writing.

The most effective preparation for any writing task is spiritual. A number of chapters in this book have emphasized this point in detail. But it's difficult to overstate this truth. Who you are inside is going to express itself in your writing. If you are dealing with unresolved spiritual struggles and are trying to hide that when you write, it will only weaken what you produce. The most effective writer is an honest writer—honest with himself or herself, honest with others, honest with God.